Breaking Controlling Powers

by
Roberts Liardon

HARRISON HOUSE
Tulsa, Oklahoma

Breaking Controlling Powers
ISBN 0-89274-495-2
Copyright © 1988 by Roberts Liardon
P.O. Box 23238
Minneapolis, Minnesota 55423

Published by Harrison House, Inc.
P.O. Box 35035
Tulsa, Oklahoma 74153

Contents

Foreword

The Apostle Paul once stated that there is nothing evil within itself; however, there is such a thing as error by excess. Error opens the door for sin. Sin then opens the door for the devil — and evil prevails.

Roberts Liardon has attempted to help people by writing this book to expose the excesses that can occur when one deals with the flesh and the devil. Thank God, through knowledge and understanding we can achieve victory over all such excesses.

In the day and age in which we live, books that tell us how to do something are very valuable. I believe that *Breaking Controlling Powers* is a valuable book, because it tells how to recognize, cope with, and be free of controlling people and controlling spirits.

Jesus said, **And ye shall know the truth, and the truth shall make you free** (John 8:32). This book will set you free!

— Dr. Doyle "Buddy" Harrison
President and Founder
Harrison House Publishers

Foreword

Positive control in the leadership of a church is a necessity. Without it, the church is like a car without a steering wheel, or a boat without a rudder. On the other hand, *negative* control causes people to become "Jesus *intimidators*" rather than "Jesus *imitators*."

Since 1981 I have had the privilege of working with many Christian ministries and churches throughout the country. Negative control is a challenge that surfaces in every Christian work I am acquainted with. In fact, the more growth, anointing, and success a ministry or church enjoys, the wider the doors seem to fly open to the potential influence of the negative side of control!

What characteristics does negative control clothe itself in? I have noticed that controllers always seem to do the following five things:

1. Controllers prefer to surround themselves with those who "need" to be controlled and are easy to control. They will use stronger people only for a season; then they readily discard them. (I call this Paper Towel Management.)

2. Controllers don't delegate responsibility easily. This allows the controller to give the impression that he is the only one who is able to do the work.

3. Controllers are good with words. They know all the Faith Movement "buzz words."

4. Controllers have memorized all the Scriptures that justify their controlling actions.

5. Controllers always think they are good managers, but they usually are not thought of as good managers by those who work for them.

Negative control can be found at every level in the organization of a church: pastor, staff, and church members alike. I even had one church client whose janitor was exercising a major negative influence in the overall atmosphere of that large church!

When kept in balance, control can be a positive force within a church. Every leader should continually examine himself to assess whether he is being a Jesus imitator or a Jesus intimidator.

> — John L. Mason
> President
> Mason and Associates
> Consultants to Management

1
What Is Control?

The power of control seems to be a problem in every time of transition from an old wave of God's glory to a new wave, such as we are experiencing today.

There is *natural* control that people can exert over others, but there is also *demonic* control that demons can exert through people over others. This book mainly deals with the abuse of control.

Christians are finally beginning to realize that what is happening in the spiritual realm is being reflected in the natural realm. For example, there is a great struggle going on in the world today for control of men's minds. This struggle is between the forces of light (Christianity) and the forces of darkness (communism and the occult).

The people of the world suffer enormously from the ungodly natural control exercised by Communist and other oppressive governments. Such governments dominate people through fear and poverty, restricting their knowledge of the world and limiting their freedoms of expression and religion.

I have traveled in 16 nations of the world, including some that are under Communist rule, so I am writing from firsthand knowledge of conditions not only in the Church world, but also in society in general.

In Communist states, I've seen people being killed because of their desire for freedom; I've seen the bread lines; and I've heard Christians in the underground churches voice the anguish of their lives.

However, people living in free societies are not immune to being controlled. This control may come from parents, spiritual leaders, spouses, friends, and from other associates, financial obligations, or even children.

One of the worst cases of control I've come across in the *spiritual* realm is the pastor who repeatedly tells his congregation, "If you'll come to my church three times a week, I believe you won't get cancer."

He's insinuating that if they *don't* come three times a week, they *will* get cancer! You'd be surprised how many people go to that pastor's church because they're afraid of getting cancer if they don't.

The Source of Control

Control does not originate in strangers; the devil does not use the beggar on the street to control your church. Please understand that.

If a stranger walked down the aisle of your church, went to the pulpit, and announced he was going to take over the service, you'd throw him out. But if someone you know and trust did the same thing, you wouldn't be so quick to ask him to sit down or leave, because of your respect for him.

You must realize that some of the people you respect right now may decide not to go on with God at some point in the future. This could cause a great problem in your life, your destiny, and your church if you are not able to discern them accurately in the Spirit.

It has become increasingly important at this point in Church history for you to know the characteristics of control and controllers.

Characteristics of Control

Let's begin this study by answering the question: What is control?

Control is when a person or persons dominate another's behavior to benefit their own personal desires and security, without any consideration toward the person they are controlling.

The three principal methods used to ensure total dominion are as follows:

1. *Emotional manipulation.* Tears, rage, and silence are the main characteristics of emotional manipulation. Silence, which is a form of rejection, is an especially powerful form of emotional manipulation.

Most people become controlled by their own emotions because they primarily make their decisions based on *feelings.* That's precisely why they make so many *wrong* decisions! In fact, most people base their decisions on feelings rather than on the safety of being led by the Holy Spirit.

That's why people end up marrying the wrong person.

That's why people in business end up making the wrong business deal, losing everything they own.

That's why some ministers pastor the wrong church. (Just because a congregation is nice does not mean you're called to pastor them! God may want you to go to Africa.)

A classic case of *emotional* manipulation starts when both sets of parents want a newlywed couple to spend the holidays with them.

It starts innocently enough when the bride mentions to her mother, "I think we're going to go see his parents for Christmas." The bride's mother starts crying, "You don't love me anymore, or you would come to *my* house for Christmas!"

This reaction throws the daughter into an emotional state. She wavers and finally agrees to go to her mother's for Christmas.

When the bridegroom calls his mother with the news, she's equally as adamant and upset. She wails, "But we had everything all planned! We can't change it now!"

Some people are controlled through these avenues of emotional manipulation. Often, if you don't agree with the controlling person, he or she starts crying, "You don't like me," or "You don't *love* me!"

Do you know what you should do at this point? Tell that person, "Well, I don't like it when you act like this, and I don't have to agree with you and be manipulated by you."

If tears won't work, often a controlling person will retreat into anger — and most people don't know how to handle someone who's angry. Do you know what to do with an angry person? Just stay calm. Look at him, state the truth, and walk out! Leave him alone with all his rage.

He won't know what to do then, so he'll probably hit the walls and beat on the chairs. Then you can go back into the room and ask, "Now, is this the action of an adult, or what? You say you've got it all together. Why did you punch a hole in my wall and beat my chair to death?"

"Because I was mad."

"Big deal. Grow up!"

Anger will monopolize the atmosphere as well as your thoughts if you're not careful. Angry words will hit your mind like machine gun bullets, preventing you from defending yourself.

If anger won't work, controlling people will use silence as a weapon. They'll shut you out. They'll just ignore you and keep you dangling — wondering. Weak people can't handle this. That's why they're able to be controlled.

For example, a pastor can be deeply hurt by a deacon or elder who resorts to this kind of manipulation. If that should happen, the pastor should remove that person from the board and sit him on the front pew until he grows up — or ask him to leave.

If a pastor is secure in what he's called to do, and his sheep are secure in God, when a guest speaker preaches the Gospel to them, it will register correctly on their spirits. They will understand what to do with the message. They won't sit there thinking, "I wonder what So-and-so thinks of this?" People who are only concerned about what someone else thinks will miss the truth they need to hear.

Don't become like this and be overly dependent on other people. If you're a dependent person, you can't enjoy normal fellowship with others, because your joy, happiness, and thoughts will come from them — not from the real you.

Remember: *The most powerful avenue by which people are controlled is emotional manipulation.* Emotional manipulation must go!

2. *Spiritual manipulation.* This includes guiding or instructing people through false visions, false prophecies, and false "words from the Lord." It also includes any kind of preaching and praying which is slanted to control rather than to edify. (Chapter 7 contains a detailed study of this subject.)

3. *Words of failure and defeat, unnatural obligation, guilt, criticism, and intimidation.* These are all used to control people's lives.

An example of words of failure and defeat used to control someone is if you tell the controller that God has called you to Africa, the controller will probably insist that God has *really* called you to Norway.

If you respond with the complete assurance of your call, "No, I'm going to Africa," the controlling type will probably reply, "Oh, well — you do whatever you want. Obey God

13

— but I doubt if you'll survive. There are diseases and wars over there, and you'll probably get sick and die."

Those words are an attack against you. Words of failure and defeat like this dominate many people's lives, and they aren't even aware of it!

Have people ever tried to intimidate you? Maybe they won't say anything. Instead, they'll give you a certain "look," or lift an eyebrow. They'll refuse to talk to you, or they'll noticeably avoid a certain topic to control you — or even make you think you're missing God.

Let's look at the case of Mr. Smith, who has a lovely family. He works for Mr. Doe, who has a horrible family (which is of his own making).

Mr. Doe forgets that Mr. Smith has a family, and he makes him work nearly round the clock. This upsets Mr. Smith, because that hurts his wife and he isn't able to spend any time with his children.

So Mr. Smith walks into his boss's office one day and announces, "I am not going to work any more overtime! I need to spend more time with my family."

Mr. Doe looks at him and purrs sweetly, "How are you doing, Smith? It's sure good to see you." Then he outlines several rush projects he wants done.

Mr. Smith crumbles. He loses all his resolve. He floats out of that office thrilled with his boss's attention, saying, "Oh, yes, sir! I'll do them for you. Yes, I understand. I'll do it."

Three minutes later, outside Mr. Doe's office, Mr. Smith is furious with himself and wonders why he crumbled to Mr. Doe's manipulation. Mr. Smith gave in because he is intimidated and able to be controlled by his boss!

Remember: Controlling spirits do not work through people you do not respect. Controlling spirits work through people you respect; people who have authority. To be free from their control, you must realize that you and a controller are both equal in God's eyes. Don't allow a controller to intimidate you.

Most of the time, when a person gets to the place where he can't handle being controlled anymore, he doesn't terminate his relationship with the controller properly. He gets very angry, fights with the controller, and ends up hurt and wounded. However, if you want to go on in the move of God, you must get rid of the negative controlling influences in your life.

2
Control in the Bible

Now let's examine the problem of control from a biblical perspective. Let's see how Jesus managed to remove Himself from people who sought to control Him.

> And when the devil had ended all the temptation, he departed from him for a season.
>
> And Jesus returned in the power of the Spirit into Galilee: and there went out a fame of him through all the region round about.
>
> And he taught in their synagogues, being glorified of all.
>
> And he came to Nazareth, where he had been brought up: and, as his custom was, he went into the synagogue on the sabbath day, and stood up for to read.
>
> And there was delivered unto him the book of the prophet Esaias. And when he had opened the book, he found the place where it was written,
>
> The Spirit of the Lord is upon me, because he hath anointed me to preach the gospel to the poor; he hath sent me to heal the brokenhearted, to preach deliverance to the captives, and recovering of sight to the blind, to set at liberty them that are bruised.
>
> To preach the acceptable year of the Lord.
>
> And he closed the book, and he gave it again to the minister, and sat down. And the eyes of all them that were in the synagogue were fastened on him.
>
> And he began to say unto them, This day is this scripture fulfilled in your ears.
>
> Luke 4:13-21

This is an interesting story. Jesus knew His destiny. He knew His call to the earth. But He didn't advertise it before it was time; He kept it within Himself and developed it.

Jesus went through His wilderness experience and *won*. Most people go into their wilderness and *stay* there. They don't get very far. The first time the devil tells them they can't succeed, they agree. "That's right," they say, and they sit down. God, however, is looking for fighters and warriors, not weak-kneed wimps — we've got enough of them already.

After Jesus emerged victorious from His wilderness experience, He walked back to His hometown, Nazareth. On the Sabbath, He entered the synagogue where He grew up.

That's where His parents "went to church." That's where the minister had trained Him as a boy. He had learned many good things from that minister.

That day, when the pastor handed the scrolls to Jesus, He opened them and read Isaiah 61:1,2. But Jesus didn't read this prophecy as a normal man would read it — as something the people expected to take place in the future. *Jesus read the prophetic passage like He owned it — because He did own it!*

Control in the Home Church

After Jesus boldly announced, **This day is this scripture** [prophecy] **fulfilled in your ears** (v. 21), the people's first reaction was, **Is not this Joseph's son?** (v. 22).

The people of Nazareth totally missed the significance of Jesus' declaration that He is the Messiah! All they could say was, "No, you can't be! You're Joseph's son."

As Jesus spoke further, calling Himself a prophet, they became incensed.

> And all they in the synagogue, when they heard these things, were filled with wrath.
>
> And rose up, and thrust him out of the city, and led him unto the brow of the hill whereon their city was built, that they might cast him down headlong.

But he passing through the midst of them went his way.

Luke 4:28-30

When you take possession of what is yours spiritually, people who are lukewarm will automatically fight you!

Jesus closed the book and handed it back to the minister. He did the right and respectful thing. He had read forcefully from it in the Spirit, but He did not try to take the meeting over. He sat down.

If Looks Could Kill...

The people were so astonished at Jesus that they did not simply *glance* at Him; their eyes were *fastened* on Him, as we saw in verse 20. This was a warlike look: a look of madness, a look of rage, a look beyond natural questioning — a look that demands to know, "Who do you think you are?"

Has anyone ever looked at you that way? If you're a true servant of God, I'm sure someone will before you die.

Notice Jesus' reply: *This day is this scripture fulfilled in your ears.* Whack!

The people stopped looking at Jesus and began murmuring to one another, "Isn't this Joseph's son?" Notice that Jesus still did not respond — and because He didn't, they wanted to destroy Him!

This was *Jesus*, the young man who grew up in their "church." This was Nazareth, one of those small towns where everyone knew everyone else's business! Everyone's kids played with Joseph and Mary's kids. And everyone supposedly loved everyone else. But not now.

The people of Nazareth wanted to kill Jesus because He did not withdraw, explain, or falter. He stood His ground.

They could not control Him! He was not under their power!

When you get to the place where people can't control you through intimidation or other means, they'll try to destroy you. They'll cast you out. In other words, they'll try to excommunicate you.

The people rose up as one to run Jesus out of town and throw Him off a nearby hilltop. This was a dramatic excommunication: They wanted to kill Him!

They were looking for the Messiah, and they thought they would recognize Him through their usual carnal ways of thinking. But they missed recognizing their Messiah! Even after all Jesus did, they still didn't believe He was the Messiah! Why? Because they were *religious* — totally in the flesh — and they did not recognize the things of the Spirit.

People who walk in the flesh don't know much about life in the Spirit. They're very unlearned; however, they think they know everything that's "religious."

Notice that Jesus did not die. He just walked through the midst of them and went on. He had a destiny to fulfill; a higher calling than they had.

Even the ones whom Jesus loved most could not control what God had called Him to do.

This is an example of a controlling spirit that operated through Jesus' "home church" to make Him back down from saying that He, the Messiah, had now come into the world and had fulfilled the prophetic Scriptures.

The Early Church Faces Control

Now let's turn to the fourth chapter of Acts, where we'll see an example of attempted control in the Early Church. We'll see how the religious leaders of Israel attempted to control the apostles Peter and John after the lame man at the Gate Beautiful was miraculously healed.

And as they [Peter and John] **spake unto the people, the priests, and the captain of the temple, and the Sadducees, came upon them,**

Being grieved that they taught the people, and preached through Jesus the resurrection from the dead.

And they laid hands on them, and put them in hold unto the next day: for it was now eventide. . . . .

And it came to pass on the morrow, that their rulers, and elders, and scribes,

And Annas the high priest, and Caiaphas, and John, and Alexander, and as many as were of the kindred of the high priest, were gathered together at Jerusalem.

And when they had set them in the midst, they asked, By what power, or by what name, have ye done this?

Then Peter, filled with the Holy Ghost, said unto them, Ye rulers of the people, and elders of Israel,

If we this day be examined of the good deed done to the impotent man, by what means he is made whole;

Be it known unto you all [not just some of you; ALL of you], **and to all the people of Israel, that by the name of Jesus Christ of Nazareth, whom ye crucified, whom God raised from the dead, even by him doth this man stand here before you whole.**

Acts 4:1-3, 5-10

That's a bold statement. Here all the religious devils in town got together to attack Peter and John for healing a sick man! This tells you that religious devils are stupid, because you shouldn't be angry when someone who was sick gets healed — you should *rejoice*!

But people who are in the flesh — people who are "religious" — don't have any common sense. They think they're on fire, but they're actually very cold. When you tell them that, or when God chooses to use someone outside of their control system, they become very angry!

21

Controlling Spirits and Religious People

Religious people have a controlling spirit, because religious spirits and controlling spirits are alike. They're twin brothers!

You'll find many controllers among people who are very religious. The others in their group are usually beaten-down sheep that they have trodden under.

But notice that Peter was not afraid to respond to strong religious people. One way to stand up to controlling devils and controlling flesh is to never fear them, and always have a spiritual response for them. Also notice that when controllers began to attack God's servants, a response to them was always recorded in Scripture.

Why were the religious leaders of Jerusalem attacking the apostles? To stop them from healing people. The leaders were afraid the healings would affect their control over people whom they thought they "owned."

Peter, being full of the Holy Spirit, explained to all of these religious leaders that healing people was a "good deed" (v. 9); not a wicked or mischievous deed.

When confronting controlling people, you need to state the truth. Don't suggest it; just state it. Peter did that. He went on to say that the healings came about . . . **by the name of Jesus of Nazareth, whom ye crucified . . . .** That's another bold statement!

Peter was addressing the same leaders who let a murderer go free in order to crucify Jesus. Peter's bold statements didn't make these controlling, religious people too happy. The leaders marvelled at the apostles, but they also made degrading statements about them:

> **Now when they saw the boldness of Peter and John, and perceived that they were unlearned and ignorant men, they marvelled; and they took knowledge of them, that they had been with Jesus.**

And beholding the man which was healed standing with them, they could say nothing against it.

But when they had commanded [That's a characteristic of control: They don't ask; they command. And there is an undercurrent of demand, causing you to feel obligated to do what they want] **them to go aside out of the council, they conferred among themselves,**

Saying, What shall we do to these men? for that indeed a notable miracle hath been done by them is manifest to all them that dwell in Jerusalem; and we cannot deny it.

But that it spread no further among the people, let us straitly THREATEN them, that they speak henceforth to no man in this name.

And they called them, and COMMANDED THEM not to speak at all nor teach in the name of Jesus.

Acts 4:13-18

Control Through Threats

Notice the phrase in verse 17, **. . . let us straitly threaten them. . . .** What does a threat do to a person? It makes him go against what he believes and submit to those who are threatening him. That's control!

The leaders threatened the apostles, **. . . that they speak henceforth to no man in this name** [the Name of Jesus]. That's control!

How did Peter and John respond in the face of these threats and commands?

But Peter and John answered and said unto them, Whether it be right in the sight of God to hearken unto you more than unto God, judge ye.

For we cannot but speak the things which we have seen and heard.

So when they had FURTHER THREATENED THEM, they let them go, finding nothing how they might punish

them, because of the people: for all men glorified God for that which was done.

Acts 4:19-21

I like these apostles! They stood their ground before all the religious devils in town. The religious people were mad because a miracle was done — and it wasn't done through them! They thought *they* should have been allowed to perform the miracle, because they were the religious rulers. However, God couldn't use them, because they were full of pride and thought they knew it all.

God isn't looking for a person who operates from his head; He's looking for someone who operates from his heart. God isn't looking for gold or silver vessels; He's looking for human beings who will be obedient. (That's why it bothers some well-educated, prideful people when God uses someone who has little or no education to be a miracle worker.)

People who are filled with pride usually criticize those who have nothing in the natural. But how can God use those who are relying on their education? *The only way an education works is if you submit it to the will of God and don't rely solely upon the education, but rely solely upon God!*

In the seventh verse, these religious leaders asked the apostles, **By what power, or by what name, have ye done this?** They were saying, "Who do you think you are, doing this without *our* permission? By whose name have you done this?"

How To Defeat Controlling Spirits

The eighth verse continues, **But Peter, filled with the Holy Ghost, said. . . .** *The only way to win over control is to be full of the Holy Spirit and power!*

In verse 10, Peter continued, "By the Name of Jesus Christ of Nazareth, whom you crucified — that's who we did it through!"

The religious leaders responded by commanding them to stop teaching and preaching, and then threatening them with everything they could think of. This reaction is a major characteristic of control even today.

3

Are You Being Controlled?

The controller and the controllee are *equally* guilty, because the controllee has to submit, and the controller has to strive in order to gain control.

Realize that *controlling spirits working through people never want you to reach your highest potential.*

A normal friend is happy when you meet his friends or other people and you start to achieve your goals. He'll encourage you. A controlling person will not. He'll say, "You can't do that. Who do you think you are?"

The greatest problem people under control have is to recognize that they are under someone's control.

How can you know if you're under someone's control?

1. You may be under someone's control if you feel physically tired and drained all the time outside your normal working hours.

You feel perfectly happy until a controlling person exerts a controlling "signal" to you by words or actions, and you suddenly become exhausted and confused.

2. You may be under someone's control if you feel as if you're running a race, but you're pulling 300 pounds behind you. You're trying to obey God, but you can't quite get it done.

Let's look at some scriptural proof.

> **While he yet talked to the people, behold, his mother and his brethren stood without, desiring to speak with him.**

> **Then one said unto him, Behold, thy mother and thy brethren stand without, desiring to speak with thee.**
>
> **But he answered and said unto him that told him, Who is my mother? and who are my brethren?**
>
> **And he stretched forth his hand toward his disciples, and said, Behold my mother and my brethren!**
>
> **For whosoever shall do the will of my Father which is in heaven, the same is my brother, and sister, and mother.**
>
> **Matthew 12:46-50**

Here Jesus' family was standing outside the crowd, waiting for special privileges. They wanted to get Jesus away from the crowd and off by themselves, so they could *control* Him.

Control by Programming

Controlling people like to get you alone with them. They like unnatural private time with you. That way, they can "program" you.

Have you ever noticed that when false people infiltrate a church, they take their little group off by themselves, and they start indoctrinating them. What are they doing? It's called programming.

You've got to watch your relationship with some of your friends and relatives: If they are not walking in the Spirit, they may end up controlling you. Certain friendships can keep you out of the glory...out of the realm of the Spirit...out of the move of God.

Carefully evaluate your relationships, even with members of your own family. Don't let anything hold you back from following God. Keep going on with God, as Jesus and Elisha did. They left their relatives (*not* spouses) behind to answer the call of God. As you follow the call of God on your life, your relatives will have to decide what they're going to do with their lives. Usually they'll follow your example and become Christians, if they love you.

All aspects of your life should be holy in the sight of God. If a friendship is not edifying to you or pleasing to the Holy Spirit, you should deal with it properly or leave it if the other person refuses to change. However, there are some relationships in life, such as marriage, where a commitment or vow has been made which should not be relinquished, and every effort must be made to work out the problem.

Why should you be so careful not to offend God? *Because Christianity is not a natural religion. It is a lifestyle; an everyday experience with God in His world.*

One of your friends or relatives may tell you, "Well, I don't think you should do that." Who asked him? Learn to quit listening to *everyone* who volunteers information.

And don't ask questions of someone who doesn't know anything about God. This is a problem with some young Christians. They often try to get information about God from people who know nothing about Him! If you want to ask a question, ask someone who knows a little more about God than you do.

3. You may be under someone's control if you feel you can't do anything without first "checking in" with that person. I'm not referring to normal respect, or letting your family or boss know where you're going to be; I'm talking about *control*. You don't have to "check in" with that many people.

There's an unnatural "checking in" that's required of you when you're under control. If you stop "checking in," your controller will claim that you're not under proper submission to his spiritual or natural authority.

4. You may be under someone's control if you feel you've lost your vision and if you're depressed much of the time. Controlling people will stop your goal and your joy in life and make their vision become your vision.

And if you're always discouraged about things — even about church — you may be under control.

Symptoms of Control

Here's another way you can tell if you're being controlled: Let's say you're having fun with your friends. You're totally happy. Then a certain person walks into the room, and you lose all your joy. You feel guilty. *You're under control!*

Also, if your mother, your father, or a friend walks into a room and you lose your joy, peace, and motivation, you'll know that something is wrong with your relationship with that person.

How can you tell if someone is trying to control you? If that person gets jealous and possessive about you and feels threatened when you start talking to other people, you're probably under the control of that person.

When you meet new friends, your controller is threatened, because the person you're meeting is taking attention away from him or her.

Yet people have a natural desire to have friends and interact with them. If someone starts interfering with that natural desire, problems will arise in a relationship.

Insecure husbands or wives may feel threatened when a member of the opposite sex starts talking to their spouse. Couples shouldn't get married until they're both secure in God and secure in themselves.

Insecure people are threatened by everything — any unusual occurrence — even the amount of money in the checkbook! Whether it's large or small, they're threatened by it. All they want is for you to be isolated in a nice little cubbyhole somewhere with them, so they can have you all to themselves.

That's the way some people are, but that's not the way God designed you to live. He designed you to have fun with Him. If you aren't having fun with God, something's wrong with your relationship with God.

Control can happen to anybody. I don't care how nice the person is, how beautiful, how rich, how important, how poor, how ugly, how mean — that person could control you.

This does not mean that you should start screaming, "I'm under control!" about every relationship after reading this book.

You must recognize that there *is* a natural flow of leadership and authority that must be respected in churches, families, and businesses. Just because your pastor, your father, or your boss asks you to do something, it doesn't mean he's trying to control you! Likewise, if the Lord has your pastor deal with you about something you're doing wrong, it doesn't mean your pastor is trying to control you.

And when your parents or spouse want to know where you're going, it's generally because they have a natural love and concern for you; it's not because they are trying to control you.

Just because you are learning about *unnatural* control doesn't mean that you should become disrespectful and forget common sense and good manners in your dealings with friends and family who *aren't* trying to control you!

This book was written to help you discern between natural authority and unnatural control; it wasn't written to instill fear in you.

The fear of being controlled is as controlling as being controlled!

There are people who break free from a situation of unnatural control of their life, but they don't recover or heal correctly afterwards. It is like having a broken limb that was not set correctly; the limb always shows evidence of the break. These people fear being controlled so much that they continue to be controlled by these fears.

You needn't go from one extreme to another. After you break free from domination by controlling spirits in people, you must face the fact that there are some *normal* and *justifiable* controlling factors in life.

What Is Justifiable Control?

Justifiable control is characterized by moderation, good, sensible regulations, and restraints that bring excitement without the abuse of one's rights.

For example, the United States Government has many controls that help protect and enhance the happiness of the American people. Examples include: (1) drug controls, (2) immigration controls, and (3) federal regulations covering such vital matters as protection of health, inspection of food, protection of natural resources, provision for education, and so forth.

The Holy Spirit is the Controller of the life of the believer. The Holy Spirit exercises His control over us by faith and love. He convicts us of areas of sin in our life.

On the other hand, a controlling spirit controls people through fear, abuse, domination, and underhanded manipulation. A controlling spirit also dominates and destroys people's joy and sense of adventure.

If you won't allow yourself to be controlled by proper moderation, regulations, and restraints, you will have problems with excesses in your life.

In conclusion, you don't have to live in the fear of control, being weak and mean because of unhealed hurts. You can be bold, strong, and compassionate by living in the liberty that God provides. Thank God, His truth has set us free!

My Prayer for You

Father, we thank You for this teaching. We do not release any condemnation on these people. We break that spirit. We break guilt. We break control off people in Jesus' Name! Give them power and authority to go on, Father. Give them strength, that they might wax so strong in the Spirit that they will last throughout eternity.

Help these people grow so they can enjoy what is due to them. In Jesus' Name, Amen.

4

What Causes Controllers?

What causes people to become controllers of others? There are a number of reasons.

1. *Hurts and wounds* is one reason why people become controllers. They vow, "I'll never get hurt like that again." They control their whole world so they won't get hurt again. Or they have been so wounded, they build a brick wall that has no door. This effectively shuts out the whole world. You've got to have a spiritual jackhammer to blast through that wall to help them.

2. Some people grew up in an atmosphere of control. *They were trained that way.* So they're just doing what they saw others do.

3. Another reason why people are in the control realm is because *they choose to be.*

Other reasons why people become controllers of others are: pride, just plain laziness (wanting everyone to serve them), jealousy, insecurities, or crises and other emotional peaks in life.

Most controllers enjoy that role, because *control serves the desires of the flesh.* Controlling other people makes controllers feel comfortable. It makes them feel like Mr. or Mrs. It!

Controlling Spouses

A characteristic of controllers is that *controllers accuse you of the things they're guilty of!*

This is especially true in cases where a battered wife starts breaking free emotionally from a controlling husband; not free from her home or the marriage, but free from control and manipulation. The husband will begin to accuse her of neglecting her duties in the home. Actually, the wife is still doing her part. However, she is now leaving her husband's normal obligations of helping in the home and helping raise the children for him to do. He senses that feeling of obligation, and he doesn't want to do it for any number of reasons.

I've been lecturing on control for some time now, and I've had some interesting reactions. Controllers do unusual things!

One man called and started out diplomatically enough, because the devil in him knew that if he were nasty, I'd hang up after telling him he needed to get delivered.

He said, "I want to discuss this topic of control with you. Ever since you started preaching it, our home has not been the same, and God is not the author of confusion."

"Well, tell me what's happening."

"My wife's not doing what she's supposed to do. She just floats around."

I asked, "What does she do?"

"Well, you know. . ."

"No, I don't. What is it?"

"She doesn't take care of the kids anymore. She says I've got to do some of it."

I said, "That sounds normal."

"But you don't understand how hard I work! Now she tells me I have to take care of certain parts of the house, like the yard, and the garage, and the cars."

I just sat there listening. I'm not making this up. I let him say enough to hang himself.

Before we ended our conversation, he was quite angry with me, because I didn't agree with his laziness. I said, "Sir, you helped bring those children into the world. Your wife takes care of the home, and that's a full-time job for her, just like your full-time job. Your pay is in dollars. Her pay is in the happiness of the home. If you don't come home and help out and add that happiness to it, there's something wrong with you.

"I know you're tired sometimes. I understand that. But you're not tired *all* the time. You feel you still have the right to go out with your friends like you did during your bachelor days. But you need to stay home more, because you're a married man now with a wife and two children."

I warned him, "If you don't start helping out in the home, when your sons turn out to be weird, don't blame your wife, because it will be *your* fault!"

He whined, "Well, I don't think you're quite getting what I'm saying."

I said, "That's right. I don't want to understand such laziness."

Controlling Friends

Control isn't limited to married couples, of course. Friends aren't immune to it, and it can lead to tragedies.

I've seen this happen with both sexes: Two young men or two young women happen to agree on something that everyone else disagrees on, so they become very close. They say to each other, "Everyone's against you, and everyone's against me, so let's stand together against the world."

Soon they get entangled. They're always seen together: When you see one, you always see the other. They're so intertwined, their identity becomes one in the eyes of other people. Each depends on the other. Insecure people can get like that. Then something negative may happen. As the friendship flows, it can even turn into a homosexual relationship.

Control by the Opposite Sex

A variation of this problem occurs between unmarried people of the opposite sex. Christians involved in a dating relationship may encounter many of the same problems with control that married couples face. A young man may be abnormally jealous, for example, or his girlfriend may be manipulative.

Another variation of control can even exist in working relationships: the pastor and his secretary, for example. It's essential to have the right people in jobs in the church office! I was sitting in one church office and heard the secretary say, "You know, pastor, your wife sure isn't *helpful,* is she?"

I've seen examples of this all over the world. What is it? It's an element of division and defilement. I wouldn't have it in my office. If my secretary said that, I would fire her on the spot.

A secretary who is a controller would say, "You need my help." Controllers always think, "You can't live without me." The point is, *they* can't live without *you*, because you're their means of security.

When you're fighting these controlling spirits, sometimes you need someone to encourage you and assure you that you're not imagining things, because controlling spirits will attempt to confuse your mind! You'll begin to think, "Is this real? My life was a lot simpler when I wasn't dealing with this."

Control eventually becomes a vicious circle of manipulation. The participants can't get away from each other. Soon they can't stand to be around each other, and this leads to conflict.

Controlling spirits must go!

5

Are You a Controller?

Learning these things about control will cause some of you to think immediately of people you know who are controllers. But what if you suspect that *you* may have a controlling personality? How can you recognize if you control people?

1. You'll know you're a controller if you feel the only way you can be important or accepted is to give orders and commands.

2. You'll know you're a controller if you feel possessive about a person or persons. . . if you feel that person has to check in with you because you know more than they do, and you know what's best for them. . . if you never accept that person's judgment of what they think they should do... and if you always belittle them, because you don't think they know anything.

Possessive people always try to make you feel like you don't know anything, you're totally ignorant and immature, and the only way you're going to make it is to check in with them and do what they say.

When you voice your opinion to them, they'll cut you down, saying, "Oh, that isn't true. I'm right. You're wrong."

One sure sign that you're a controller is when you never allow any differing opinions or ideas to be voiced, accepted, or even discussed. The other person's voice goes in one ear and out the other, and you go back to doing your own thing.

3. You'll know you're a controller if you feel jealousy toward a person.

For example, if the person you are controlling starts talking to someone else, you'll automatically feel jealous and possessive, and you'll try to cut that relationship off. You'll probably walk over and get into the conversation to monitor it!

Control Through Religious Domination

Religious people do that a great deal. *Religious controlling people don't want you to get around people who are so secure and strong that they can't be dominated.* And they especially don't like secure, strong preachers who can't be dominated.

I've had religious controllers try to interrupt my sermons! Once when I was in North Carolina, minding my own business, preaching nicely about the end times, a man stood up and demanded, "Who do you think you are? (They always ask me that question!) I want to hear the Word; not your opinion."

Now, there was a challenge — and I love challenges! However, the middle of my sermon wasn't the right time for a discussion. What happened was that he got irritated because he couldn't put his two cents' worth in when I attacked his unscriptural pet doctrines. (I love doing that.) So he was no longer in control, and he had the nerve to stand up and try to dominate my whole sermon.

I told him to stop talking and sit down. I wasn't going to let the devil say his thing.

He replied, "I want to say what I have to say."

I said, "You're not going to say it in my meeting." I told the ushers, "Take him out."

Was that rude? No. He didn't respect the chain of command of that church; he didn't obey the flow of the Holy Spirit. He was reacting out of defensiveness, not humility.

When Control Is Necessary

Some may argue, "You're mean." You go ahead and let people do whatever they want to while *you're* trying to preach, and see how far you get. You'll see how much the Holy Spirit will visit you — He won't visit you at all!

"Well, you're certainly opinionated."

No, I'm just secure in knowing what's really happening on the earth today. I'm on a road that is going to take me to places where dramatic events will occur. I'm on a road that many of you need to get on.

Perhaps some of you are already on this road, but demonic forces are fighting you. If so, just keep fighting. You'll win. Don't give up, because this struggle is going to end in glory. It's going to be wonderful. It's going to be fun!

One of the problems in the Church world today is that Christians don't understand authority. They don't have a chain of command. They only understand *permissiveness*. They say, "You do whatever you want to. It's fine with me. Let's all walk in love."

Do you know what they're walking in? They're walking in jeopardy. They're in danger of losing everything they have!

How To Confront Demons

In the days to come, devils are going to confront you like never before, and they're not always going to confront you behind closed doors; they're going to confront you in public.

They're going to let you have it, because they're going to see the glory on you, and it's going to scare them. When devils are scared, some will run off, but others will attack to see if you'll back down and lose what you have.

41

Some will see if you'll have a discussion with them. When they start losing the battle, controlling people always want to discuss it! They want you to sign a treaty with them.

You don't have treaties with the devil. The Bible says you're to CAST him out; not DISCUSS him out.

God is looking for a group of people who will love, respect, and obey His commands, not for those who will do their own thing.

4. You'll know you're a controller if you feel threatened over new relationships this person has or finds.

You are a controller if you feel your friendship and communication with another person are threatened when that person speaks to someone else, prays with them, goes out for dinner or some other activity with them, or basically spends more than five minutes with them.

Commitment Isn't Control

This discussion is limited to people in friendships, not people in marriages. Married people's best friends should be their mates. A married couple has made commitments to each other in the sight of God and man. A certain amount of exclusiveness is an implied part of marriage.

A married man, for example, is to leave his parents and cleave only to his wife, the Bible says: **Therefore shall a man leave his father and his mother, and shall cleave unto his wife; and they shall be one flesh** (Gen. 2:24).

This doesn't say he's to remain a "mama's boy" and go to his mother's house for dinner every night. Nor does it say that he's to hang out with his old crowd every night of the week. He's a married man now, and he has responsibilities toward his wife.

When the couple has children, the husband's responsibilities increase to include them, for now he must help his wife rear them in the fear and admonition of the Lord, as the Bible teaches.

A married man, for example, has no business going off and socializing unduly, dating, or having dinner with a woman who isn't his wife or close relative. Why? Because he is to cleave only to his wife! (The only exception might be a business meeting over a meal, preferably with others present and definitely with his spouse's knowledge.)

A married man should remember that his Christian wife is not only his mate; she is *also* his sister in Christ, and therefore entitled to even more consideration and courtesy! Her concern for his well-being should not be mistaken for control.

Furthermore, this discussion must not be mistaken as an excuse for spouses to seek inappropriate relationships outside of their marriages. Married men with roving eyes have always used the excuse "She doesn't understand me" to seek relationships with other women.

The teachings found in this book are not meant to give anyone an excuse in any way to label their spouse as a controller and seek other relationships or terminate their marriage!

5. You'll know you're a controller if you feel you must protect that person from every experience. The reason is because the thing he wants to do threatens your time with him.

You must understand that a controlling person thinks, lives, and "eats" the other person all the time. If anything keeps that person from spending time with the controller, the controller will attack it and attempt to get rid of it as quickly as he can. He will go to any length or any expense to make sure the person he's controlling will spend the majority of his time with him.

Control Leads to Domination

He'll dominate that person's vacations, dates, marriage, jobs, home-buying, church-going, or even setting up a bank account. *A controller will dominate every area of your life if you allow it.*

If you're not careful, you can get so entwined with a controller that, in extreme cases, it will take years to get out of the relationship.

6. You'll know you're a controller if you react in an unnatural way to statements made about the person you're controlling.

For example, if someone makes a positive statement about the person you control, you automatically criticize the controlled person to make sure no friendship will occur.

On the other hand, if someone makes a negative statement about you, the controller, you will immediately defend yourself with a positive statement to make yourself look good.

7. You'll know you're a controller if you are over-protective.

How Control Hinders God's Spirit

Elders and deacons may be so overprotective of their church that they won't allow the pastor to flow under the anointing, and they won't help him do what the Lord has told him to do.

Overprotection means that they're controlling the pastor and the church. If they do not recognize the hindrance this causes to the work of God, they need to be removed from their position.

"But they've been elders for 14 years."

That's the reason there's been no move of God in the church for 14 years!

If you really want the move of God, you're going to have to pay a price for it. If you want "God unlimited," you're going to have to pay a price that's unlimited. Many things that people call dear are going to have to go. *There will have to be many changes in some churches before the glory of God manifests there.*

8. You'll know you're a controller if you make plans for the person you control without his or her permission.

A controller will do this. If the person who is being controlled doesn't want to go along with the plan, he feels so guilty that he ends up doing it anyway. (He also knows that if he doesn't go along with it, all hell will break loose!)

Has a relative ever volunteered your services on a certain project without your permission? If you don't do it, there will be war in the family for weeks. That's control, and many families are so controlled that they never enjoy a normal life.

God didn't design you to live a miserable life under someone else's plans and desires for your life. You were meant to live your own life with God. If anyone thinks he or she has a right to control your life in order to make you successful, that's a lie.

If deacons and elders think they can do whatever they want to, ordering the pastor around, they've got another thought coming; especially when they stand before God.

He's going to say, "Why didn't you let that pastor flow in the Spirit and let my Spirit manifest?"

"But God, we *thought* we were doing the right thing."

They never prayed; they never read the Word; they never considered God's opinion.

Selfishness in Control

Controllers do everything for their own gain, their own security, their own popularity, and their own praise. Even if they tack some humble words onto a prideful statement, there's still the underlying current, "I did it."

9. You'll know you're a controller if you criticize every move and every statement the other person makes.

You will even use Scripture out of context in order to keep people under your authority. That's the way some intercessors control people in the church. That's the way some pastors control their sheep.

10. You'll know you're a controller if you think the person you control owes you something, and you demand that he pay you back.

For example, Mom and Dad have a son, Rick, who has been a very good son. He hasn't been rebellious. Rick feels a call to the ministry, but because he enters Bible school or seminary instead of engineering school, his parents have a fit. They want him to have "security" in life.

They nag, cry, interfere, and generally do everything they can to get Rick to change his mind, leave the seminary, return to his hometown, and enroll at State University uptown. (They want him to live at home, of course, so they can continue to control him.) They stress their belief that he "owes" them this consideration because they're his parents and they have devoted their lives to rearing him.

The Call vs. Control

They fail to see that the call of God on Rick's life is the highest calling there is in life! Rick must follow Elisha's advice, kiss his parents good-bye respectfully, and follow God.

When Lester Sumrall was a teenager and left his parents' home in Florida to preach, his father was enraged and predicted that Lester would starve to death. Lester's heavenly Father has taken excellent care of him these many years!

11. You'll know you're a controller if you control people with flattery.

This is the way some ministries grow. The preacher not only controls his people through flattery; he also gets money out of them through flattery!

These preachers say, "Oh, you're so wonderful! God loves you."

Everyone knows that.

Yet they won't help the girl who has had an abortion, and they won't cast the homosexual demon out of anyone. They don't want such people in their church, because they're not "nice."

12. You could have a controlling spirit if you begin to have romantic feelings toward someone who is a member of your same sex, because the homosexual spirit is a very dominant spirit. It likes to bring people under control for its own selfish purposes.

In conclusion, you probably have a problem with control if your life *totally revolves* around nurturing and developing another human being.

Your personal security shouldn't even depend on your spouse or your children; it should depend on God.

Being secure with God will enhance your other relationships.

We can't expect the glory of God to fall and the Book of Acts to continue in our age if everyone is trying to control everyone else!

We need to get on our faces before God and cry out to Him. We must give our all to God if we want *His* all. It's not some of self and some of God; *it's none of self and all of God.*

6

Control by Parents

As we have seen, controlling spirits try to work most often through people closest to you — even family — rather than through strangers.

The *normal* control in a family situation — such as the normal control the Bible says a parent is to exercise over a child — can be abused and can become unnatural.

Adults in a family can consciously or unconsciously limit a young person's ability to succeed in life because of negative and even unscriptural family attitudes or "customs." In 1 Timothy 1:4, Paul said that "endless genealogies" should be avoided. "Endless genealogies" can be *boundaries* and *limitations* one inherits from his family's philosophy and traditions.

Some examples are:

1. "No one in this family may ever buy a new car; only a used car."

2. "No one in this family may ever leave our church or denomination, because our grandfather helped lay the foundation of it."

3. "No one in this family may marry without the approval of their relatives; they may not follow their own heart."

"Endless genealogies" often become controlling factors in the way people live and train their children. However, Christian couples should not rear their children this way. Christian couples need to break away from these ungodly hindrances and limitations and train their children in the victory and likeness of Christ!

The Case of the Overprotective Mother

As an example of control by a parent, let's look at the case of the overprotective mother. A young woman and a young man were born into average homes. Their parents loved them, like all parents should. However, the girl's mother overdid it: She was an overprotective mother. (An overprotective parent is one who wants to know everything about their child from A to Z — and beyond Z — and also control that child's life.)

This mother's whole life revolved around her daughter — which set the stage for major problems later. (We're using a mother to illustrate this story, but it's not unusual for some fathers to behave the same way.)

The young woman and the young man grew up and went away to college, where they met and started dating. Then they got engaged. Both families prayed and felt the engagement was of God, so they gave it their blessings.

This is the way Christians should act. If a romantic attachment is *not* of God, don't say, "I do," or one day you'll say, "Why did I say it?" If it *is* the will of God, go for it, and enjoy God's blessings!

When You Shouldn't Marry

Don't marry someone just because your soulish nature likes his big muscles or her beautiful blue eyes. *Don't marry until God says that person is the one for you!*

The two young people in our story were meant to be married; their marriage was of God. Their families recognized it, and it was a blessed coming together. So the couple got married, went on their honeymoon, and established their first home.

For a while everything went smoothly, but then the bride's mother started to interfere. She had given her whole life to rear that daughter. When the girl got married and left home, part of that mother's security seemed to disappear.

Sometimes when the mother of the bride cries her eyes out at the wedding, it's not because she's happy; it's because her secure little world has crumbled! She has lost the person on whom she had based her whole security, and she doesn't know what to do anymore. She becomes deeply depressed.

The Controlling Power of Words

The mother in our story, however, knew that she hadn't lost *everything* yet, because she still had the power to influence her daughter's life, consciously or unconsciously, with her *words*. Therefore, she began to go to the newlyweds' home on invited — and uninvited — visits.

She was polite for the first five minutes, but then she began to strongly state her opinions on every subject. She didn't realize that her parental authority had been broken. She didn't realize that she had no right to step in with her advice unless the couple asked for it.

Her first attack — *a guilt trip* — went something like this:

"Don't you know who I am? I'm your mother! I brought you into this world. Now you don't respect me!"

On a later visit, she tried *self-pity*. She was more threatened by the young husband by now, so she cried and said, "You've *rejected* me. You don't *love* me anymore! You shouldn't buy this car. You shouldn't do this. You shouldn't do that. You'd better listen to me, because I know what's best for you!"

This caused great emotional upheaval in the daughter. She finally gave in and said, "All right, Mother. We'll do it your way."

The young husband came home from work as usual. He was accustomed to being met with a kiss. That day he was met by an enraged wife who said, "Mom was here today. We have to do this, this, and this. . ."

It caught him totally off guard. He tried to be nice and respectful, and he obliged for a season — but when he couldn't stand it anymore, he said, "No."

Control Drives a Wedge

When the daughter began to pamper her mother, she was no longer siding with her husband, and a wedge was driven into their relationship. In the beginning of their marriage, the couple had had a mutual agreement. Now that the mother had interfered, the couple was at war.

The newlyweds fought during the next few days. The bridegroom said, "Why doesn't your mother stay home?" The bride replied, "You just don't like my mother!" And the war continued. It took the couple two days to pray and talk together, recognize their love for each other, and get into harmony again.

Then the bride's mother came over again on an uninvited visit to see if her orders were being carried out. This time the bridegroom was home, so she told him he was no good; he had broken up the family; and he wasn't the one her daughter should have married — she had missed God. This episode threw the daughter into total emotional depression.

What was it? *It was control over the daughter.*

A Time for Parents To Let Go

Ecclesiastes says there is a time for everything. *There is also a time for parents to let go of their married children and respect their marriage!*

When parents won't do this, it causes major problems. When parents visit the newlyweds and tell them what they should do, it causes problems. When grandchildren are born and grandparents start telling the parents how to rear these children, it causes even more problems.

When a young couple asks their parents or in-laws for advice, they should give it, but if they don't ask, the parents should keep quiet and pray! But most parents can't wait for someone to ask; they just barge in and tell the couple how to live.

Parental interference causes *friction* in their children's marriages, and that's how some *marital problems* begin.

The tragedy is, some marriages never survive this interference, because one of the partners is unable to break a parent's control over his or her life.

So some divorces are actually *caused* by interfering parents!

I'm not saying that every in-law is a potential problem, but in-laws who attempt to control their children do cause problems. The most prevalent in-law problem is found in controlling parents who won't release their daughter or son. They haven't trusted their own training of that child.

It's not that they're really concerned; *the problem is that their security is vested in that daughter or son.* When their child is out on his own, it causes the parents to realize that their security, which was in that child, is now lost — and they don't know what to do. They're living in such insecurity, they go into a frenzy!

When controlling people lose their hold over the controlling victim, they'll go into a frenzy and do anything to grab back their control! That's why the in-law wars get very dramatic!

7

Control by Church Members

Parental control and manipulation are similar in many ways to the *spiritual control and manipulation* that can occur among church members (including preachers), who are members of another family — God's family.

Unfortunately, there are those in the church who "lord it over" others because they feel they hold a higher position. For example, those who are chosen to be deacons and elders may become pious and standoffish instead of becoming servants to all.

Then there are those upon whom God has bestowed an anointing or gift. This may make them feel they are among the elite, so they carry an air of untouchableness about them. They look down on people and often use them instead of loving and caring for them.

They fail to realize that a strong, godly character helps their gift or anointing to operate at its full potential and last a lifetime. Those who don't build a strong character may lose what they have.

God is a personal God who speaks to men's and women's hearts individually. Believers who are in leadership roles must be particularly careful to say *exactly* what the Lord says — nothing more and nothing less! Leaders have a responsibility to be certain that when they say something is of God, it really is. They do this by prayer, searching the Scriptures, and seeking seasoned, godly counsel.

A problem that surfaces in many churches and ministries is when those in leadership decide to undertake a project without consulting heaven. Instead, they use their position to tell their people, "God said I was to do this" when God did not say anything of the sort. This seeming blanket approval from heaven for their pet projects successfully stifles any opposition or questioning.

This may be an ego problem, and it may be used as a form of control. It needs to be discussed in this hour when men forsake heaven to have Hollywood.

Prefacing all remarks with "the Lord told me" frees a pastor to engage in all kinds of business dealings, building programs, missionary projects, or even radio and television outreaches — *whether or not God wants that church to engage in these things!* And it makes the pastor seem to be *extremely* spiritual. After all, doesn't he hear from heaven on his very own "hot line"?

Yet we must understand that there *are* times when God does speak specifically about situations in the church or ministry that need to be dealt with. But we will know that it's God by our inward witness; not by our soulish feelings, according to Romans 8:16.

Another ego trap ministers fall into is manipulating a congregation (especially the young people) into frequent, emotional "altar calls" to rededicate their lives.

When this happens every Sunday night, it can cause the young people to question their salvation! It stunts their spiritual growth and excitement. They are never able to stop **...laying again the foundation of repentance from dead works, and of faith toward God** (Heb. 6:1). But it "proves" to the pastor what a powerful speaker he is and how well he can control his people.

This does not mean that altar calls for salvation or recommitment should cease, but the same people do not need to recommit themselves week after week!

Control by the Superspiritual

Those of us who grew up in the church are well acquainted with Sister Know-It-All. She represents probably the simplest kind of spiritual control in a church. She's the one who shouts the loudest and wants everyone to obey her, because she's convinced she's the most spiritual person in the church.

Today, many intercessors believe that *they* are the most spiritual people in the church, and they try to use their position to control the pastor, even though he is in the fivefold ministry and they are only in the ministry of helps.

Pastors must not be afraid to confront intercessors and tell them to pray decently and in order or go sit down for a while until they become normal again. (This is not an attack against real intercessors.)

Closely related to the superspiritual intercessors is Mrs. Vision, who always has a morbid word for you. She says she saw you on a black mountain that fell into a black river. According to her, this means you're going to die!

The truth is, she didn't have a visitation from God; she just dreamed this up because you won't go to Africa like she wants you to!

That's one way controlling people try to get you: They act very spiritual. They act like they're important spiritual people. I don't care *who* they are. I don't care if they're Mr. Big It. Their control is of the devil!

Control by Spiritual Gifts

Unfortunately, some people even misuse spiritual gifts in their attempt to control others.

This is how tongues and interpretation and prophecy can be used for spiritual manipulation: Suppose we're in a lively Gospel meeting. Everyone's rejoicing and shouting. Someone raises his hands and yells, *"Thus saith the Lord..."* He then delivers a supposed prophecy.

(In the most extreme cases, this can get over into the dangerous realm of personal prophecy, where people are given directions on whom to marry, and so forth.)

Everyone in that wild meeting screams, "Yes!" But your spirit says, "No!" And if you aren't strong in the Spirit, you'll be swayed by these hyperflesh believers.

Many of the things that people label "spiritual" actually come from the mental realm. You'll know whether it's of God or not if it's pointed toward *self*. If a person's "revelation" — or even prophecy — benefits or points to him, it's not of God.

Notice, too, that a controlling person's security is always centered in another person — another self — not in God. If you don't do what that person says, his world falls apart! *And insecure people can become very vicious when their desires are thwarted.*

Controlling Prayers

Another variation of spiritual manipulation is *controlling prayers*. They're a mild form of witchcraft! Can Pentecostal people, Word of Faith people, Baptist people, Methodist people, and other Christians pray controlling prayers? Certainly.

A controlling prayer is composed of words spoken with a spiritual force behind them by a person who understands what he or she is doing in the spiritual realm. Such a prayer is when a person prays *his own human desires or will for you out of his human heart,* trying to make you obey his desires rather than the Lord's desires for your life.

In other words, through his prayers in the spiritual realm, he uses spiritual influences to control your natural life for his own benefit. Don't forget: *Words are weapons in the realm of the Spirit!* (Prov. 18:21; Matt. 12:37.)

An example of controlling prayer is the woman who doesn't approve of the girl you're dating. She wants you to marry her daughter, so she prays and prays that you won't marry the other girl. It's a controlling prayer — and all of it is witchcraft in a minor form.

What is witchcraft? It's the attitude, "You live or die because I say so." It's curses. What are curses? Words spoken against you on behalf of someone else's desires.

Warfare With Mature Spiritual Beings

Know this: *As you go higher in God, this spiritual warfare gets vicious, because you are no longer dealing with immature spiritual beings.* You are dealing with mature spiritual beings on both the negative side of darkness and the positive side of light.

Many ministers think they know everything there is to know about this kind of spiritual warfare, but the sad truth is that they don't know anything about it. *They can't even get control of their own church or organization!*

The man with the $1,000 offering *owns* them. He doesn't believe anyone should dance in the Spirit, so they stop the whole service if someone does. That's financial manipulation.

Church members also use unnatural obligation to control their pastor. They say, "You're *obligated* to do this, because I gave you $1,000."

You owe no man anything; you're only indebted to the Lord. Unnatural obligation must go!

Catering to the Flesh

The main reasons why many people will not go forward in this new move are because the manifestation of the glory of God is not catering to their flesh, or else they don't want to offend anyone.

Psalm 119:165 says, **Great peace have they who love Your law; nothing shall offend them or make them stumble** (*The Amplified Bible*). If you're easily offended, it's one way you can know you're in the flesh! If someone can raise an eyebrow and offend you, you're not very strong in the Spirit, my brother and sister.

We're not discussing just being born again; we're discussing Christian maturity. Maturity does not always come by saying the things people's ears want to hear. If that's what you do, all you'll get is "itching ears" instead of hearing ears.

God is not looking for preachers who are afraid of other preachers, boards, congregations, or denominations. He's looking for sergeants who will train men and women of God to endure the storms of life totally unafraid.

We must learn to flow in the Spirit the way God established in the New Testament. We must be in the Spirit to be a part of this new move of God. We must become secure in God and free from control.

A Word to Pastors

Pastors must learn to flow with God and other preachers, because when pastors become insecure, they start fighting and bickering.

The only reason why a pastor won't stand up and say what he believes is because he's controlled. A piece of paper saying he's a "reverend" often stops him from obeying God. Who cares about a piece of paper that says you're a reverend? God ordains you in heaven. That's enough.

What's more important — obeying God or obeying some man who *thinks* he's God? You must decide that.

Unnatural submission is a part of religious politics. *Religious politics is nothing but devilish control in the church and a false sense of power.*

We're in a war! You don't have time to have your own way! You don't have time to go the way of a controlling personality or a controlling denomination. You only have time to go God's way!

Some people say if you advocate such an attitude, you're being disrespectful or rebellious. No, you're just refusing to be controlled by a bunch of controlled people.

They'll call you a rebel. You're not; you're free. You're in right relationship with God. They'll say you're in pride. They'll say you're too hard. They'll say you're not submissive. They'll say you're preaching error. These accusations come because your strength, freedom, joy, and success challenge their insecure lifestyle, beliefs, and status.

There is no way you can have decent fellowship with other ministries unless they are secure and have their own relationship with God. If they're dependent on someone to tell them what to do, and you're secure, a major conflict could start between you. Also, they could make slanderous statements against you, because insecure people are threatened by everything and everyone.

Insecure people will always accuse you of being in pride. They will say, "Why are you so absolute? Why are you so strong in your beliefs? There's something wrong with you." No, it's because you're secure and they're insecure.

Insecure people always want to live in wonderland: They wonder this and they wonder that. Secure people know themselves and their God.

What Christianity Really Is

I can go to a church, deliver the word of the Lord, and flow in the gifts of the Spirit — *but dramatic manifestations are not typical of what Christianity is all about.* Christianity includes learning basic scriptural truths and developing enough character to avoid the trite expression, "I'm walking in love," when what you're really feeling is just human sympathy.

When someone is secure enough in God to admit this, many people are ready to accuse him of not walking in love. They want him to wallow in human sympathy with them!

Human sympathy says, "You've got a problem. Let's get in the ditch and wallow around in the mud together."

The love of God says, "All right, there is a problem here. This is the way out. Come on." This is the love of God. God doesn't always speak what you want to hear; He speaks the truth.

Lack of Respect

Yes, there is a problem in the modern Church concerning lack of respect for authority. *There is no respect for the authority of the Holy Spirit, and there is no respect for God Himself!*

People say that they love God, but they break His laws every day of the week and think He's going to approve of their actions. An example of this was a sick man in Missouri who wanted me to pray for him. The power was there to heal him, so I began to lay hands on the man.

The Holy Spirit said, "Don't touch him!" I thought that was the devil, so I went ahead and tried to lay hands on him again. The Holy Spirit said, "I said, 'Don't touch him!' He's unclean."

I thought, "What is going on?" I said, "Lord, what is the problem here?"

He said, "This man commits willful adultery with his next-door neighbor's wife."

God showed me the house. I saw the man walk through the front door. I could have told him which bedroom he was in. The woman's husband works on Saturday mornings. That's when this man visits her.

The Holy Spirit said, "Tell him to repent, and I'll heal him immediately." (1 John 1:9.)

I thought, "Well, he might be happy to do that."

I took my microphone off so no one could hear me. I said, "The Lord tells me you're committing adultery."

He said, "That's right." The casual way he admitted it shocked me.

"You're in adultery, and God can't heal you unless you get out of it and repent right now."

Then he got mad at me. He said, "I have repented. I repent *every time* I go out the front door after doing it, and I'm perfectly fine. I'm still growing spiritually. I have not lost an ounce of anything." That's what he said.

I thought, "This man has lost his mind!"

Problems in the Church

This *catering to the flesh* is one of the major problems we're seeing in the modern Church.

Another problem is a *lack of commitment*. There is a lack of commitment to clean the church building or help the pastor.

There's also a lack of *commitment to prayer*. Where is everyone when the church is under attack? Why don't the people gather at the church on Saturdays or before the services and break the power of the devil?

Everyone thinks the pastor should do all the praying for the church. No, no, no — *you* are supposed to pray too. *You* are supposed to help in the Kingdom of God.

"Well, I'm too busy."

Then you could be a backslider. Are you in the Kingdom or aren't you? Are you just walking around wearing a nametag that says, "Born Again, Spirit Filled"? Do you live the life? I don't want to hear any excuses on this subject. It's between you and God.

Usually after I make that statement about prayer from the pulpit, everyone wants to explain to me why they can't pray. I don't want to hear it! If you really love God, you'll find time for Him! *You always find time to do whatever you really like.*

You found time for dating in college, and you were busy. You found time to go buy a car on Saturday, and you were busy. You found time to watch a football game on Sunday afternoon.

An Urgent Message

The times are so grave, I can no longer present a nice little Gospel message to God's people. I believe that many men and women of God, if they're really in the flow of the Holy Spirit, sense this same urgency.

These are the last days. We don't have time to wait six months for you to decide to be spiritual (and just because you go to church and pray in tongues does not mean you're spiritual — you can be backslidden with tongues coming out of your mouth)!

Most people consider you to be backslidden if you commit adultery or fornication, stop going to church, stop reading the Bible, and/or watch dirty movies. That's probably quite true, but if you want to get closer to home, I believe that *being backslidden is when you lose your hunger for the things of God,* and you lack the desire to press closer into God than you are right now.

You see, living in the Spirit takes more than just being nice, going to church, and acting spiritual. *You have to be spiritual.*

Some people are frightened of *being spiritual* because they have been criticized and rejected, but they must get healed of their wounds so they can be what God has called them to be.

Why were they wounded? *Because when you get spiritual, all the carnal people will fight you!* They don't want to pay the price to get what you have or *more* than you have.

That's why some pastors won't allow their people to go further in the gifts of the Spirit or further in the move of the Holy Spirit. They don't want their sheep to go across town and enjoy a service in another church. Therefore, these pastors warn their flock, "If you go to another church, you'll get *devils!* You'll get this and you'll get that." That's control!

Some denominations will not allow their members to go deeper into the things of the Spirit. They label these people devil-conscious fanatics and everything else. Yet the truth is, the accusers are carnal and the people they're accusing are usually spiritually in tune.

These denominations will even call a committee meeting and pull the papers on the minister or the church that dares to move on with God. (Then they'll spread the word that this person or church is no good.) This is actually the work of controlling spirits who are out to kill a move of God in the church.

Control by Friends

Friends will attempt to exercise spiritual manipulation in much the same way. For example, let's suppose there are two families from the same church — it can be a Baptist church, Methodist church, or Pentecostal church — and they are good friends.

Then one of the families gets turned on to the things of God. They're no longer lukewarm and backslidden; they're moving on with God. They decide to go to a spiritual church across town. There the Word is preached without compromise, worship and praise are directed to God Himself, the presence of the Holy Spirit is evident in every service, and quality fellowship is enjoyed among the church members.

The family that's still attending the "respectable" church gets angry. They accuse their friends of attending a church that's weird — if not occult. "They've got devils!" they say.

Because the family that's on fire is young in the Lord and doesn't know much — and because they believe that their denominational friends are such great spiritual leaders (not realizing that they're backslidden) — they submit because of fear. At times they even feel guilty for desiring such moves of God.

Because of their intense spiritual hunger, they sneak across town for special meetings when their friends are out of town. At these times, the hungry family comes totally alive.

But when their friends return home, the hungry family keeps quiet so no one will know what they're doing. They don't want to be confronted, because they don't know how to handle the situation.

What is this? It's control!

"But, I don't want to *offend* people," most of you will say.

Well, do you know whom you offend when you don't want to offend man? *You offend God!*

"What do you mean?"

I mean, your carnal attitudes toward people have to go, because your spiritual life has room in it just for you and God!

Control by Intimidation

Preachers, never be intimidated by any other preacher in the world. I don't care how big his or her ministry is. I don't care what he's supposed to have done for God. I don't care who he is or where he comes from: Don't you ever dare be intimidated by him!

If the President of the United States comes to your house, preacher, tell him exactly what God told you to tell him and do exactly what God told you to do. Don't be afraid; just dare to enjoy it!

Young apostles and prophets: Don't you ever dare let a misinformed person tell you you can't obey God while you're still young!

Young married couples: Don't you ever dare let other married couples tell you that you have to have marital problems. You *don't* have to. Just because the couple who has been giving you this bad advice has been married unhappily for 50 years doesn't mean that you have to be unhappy too!

Not everyone who speaks has something to say! We need to pray that some people's mouths will be closed for a while. It's true! Sister Bucketmouth is one who needs that prayer. She thinks she has to tell everyone everything about everybody. Do you know what that's called? Gossiping and backbiting. And do you know what God says about it? He hates it.

God Is Cleansing His Church

God is cleansing His Church. Look at Ephesians 5:27.

> **That he might present it [the Church] to himself a glorious church, not having spot, or wrinkle, or any such thing; but that it should be holy and without blemish.**

What are the spots and blemishes? What are the wrinkles? What are these things?

A glorious church is one whose members flow in harmony with each other. A glorious church is one where there is no competition, no threat, no disrespect — only understanding and teachableness, flowing in the highest degree, and stretching for more of God.

A glorious church is one that is not in competition with the church across town, *even if that church is in competition with you.*

A glorious church is one whose members are not trying to dominate each other and try to win the rank of being the best or the most superspiritual one in the church.

8

Control by Money

The old saying goes, "He who pays the piper calls the tune." There is a great deal of truth to this saying, of course.

A number of people will be able to control you through money during your lifetime. It starts when you are a child. Your parents exerted a certain amount of control over your behavior through your allowance. You probably were expected to perform certain tasks around the house, in the yard, or on a farm, if you lived on one, in exchange for your allowance.

Later in your life, your bosses exerted a great deal of control over your behavior and job performance through your salary. These kinds of control using money are normal, as long as they are not excessive in any way.

Parents — particularly well-to-do parents — also use money as a means to control adult children. Spouses, too, use money as a lever of control; especially at the present time, when both partners in a marriage usually work.

A controlling influence that may never have occurred to you is *debt*. Being in debt means that you are to some extent under the control of other people. Debts can restrict the joy and achievement level of people's lives — and the pressure of being in debt can wreck marriages!

In this hour of a shaky economy, we must operate totally by God's laws of giving and receiving. (Luke 6:38.) Remember: *God's kingdom never suffers!* Be wise in your financial and business dealings so that you and your family can enjoy your life on God's beautiful earth without the restraints of debt.

Meet Mr. Big Bucks, the Controller

The above examples of financial control are common and often discussed. However, we'll consider control through money in a far different way: as it affects the local church. We'll study Mr. Big Bucks, a prominent member of the church. He's *really* into control! (And unfortunately, his type is frequently found in churches.)

Mr. Big Bucks thinks that because he gives large tithes and offerings, he has the right to issue orders. If everyone doesn't do *exactly* what he wants, and if the service doesn't end *exactly* at noon, he blows up at the pastor and threatens to reduce or withhold his offerings.

If that pastor is not strong, and if his security is in Mr. Big Bucks, he will quickly buckle under this financial pressure and agree to do anything the man wants — without praying first or discussing it with the Lord — just to keep that large tithe! In other words, that pastor is depending on flesh instead of on God.

Who does Mr. Big Bucks think he is, dictating to the pastor what to do? *Jesus is the Head of the Church!*

Mr. Big Bucks needs to learn that you don't give money into the church so you can become puffed up; you give money to God because you *love* Him!

When I start preaching this, people who are acting as controllers of others begin to react immediately. I mean — *immediately!* They'll start trying to intimidate me with threatening looks. Then they'll try to find something wrong with me — the way my hair is cut, the clothes I wear — anything.

"Who does he think he is, coming in telling me all this?" they demand.

I'm a servant of the Most High God; that's who I am. You don't intimidate me. I got delivered from intimidation a long time ago!

Buying a Role in the Service

Often these well-to-do church members use the fact that they are the biggest tither as a lever to sing a certain song, dance in the Spirit, give a message in tongues, or even prophesy at a certain point in the services.

They think the amount of their giving guarantees them this privilege, whether they're in the Spirit or in the flesh. If a speaker comes to that church and discerns that Mr. Big Bucks is in the flesh and prevents him from operating, he'll march straight to the pastor and threaten, "Pastor, if you don't do something about that, I'll just have to keep some of my money out next time the offering bucket comes around." This is control, and it must go!

One thing God carefully trained me in at the very beginning of my ministry is not to depend on people's giving to pay my ministry's bills.

God's got gold streets in heaven! I don't need Mr. Big Bucks's $20. If he wants to give it, fine; if he doesn't, it doesn't bother me. I refuse to get into bondage to the money syndrome.

Control Hinders the Flow of the Spirit

A frequent problem in the modern Church is that most preachers *are* dependent upon the people's giving. They get so controlled by money that they lose the real flow of the Spirit!

This is one reason why some congregations are not going on with God. A few people with controlling spirits are running things, and the pastor doesn't want to lose them, because they're influential in that town. However, their control will stop the move of God in that church!

Pastors also have a need to be liked. They want to have public opinion on their side. When they should be preaching the sermon God told them to preach, they preach another sermon, because they don't want to offend their influential, well-to-do members. These pastors want a big church — but by compromising, they miss having a church that is filled with the glory of God!

This must change! In this new wave, we're going to see who's real and who's not. Those who aren't real will try to stop those of us who are, but the glory will take care of those who oppose us.

A minister must realize that God is his Source; not Mr. Big Bucks. What a pastor should do in this situation is say, "Brother Big Bucks, here's your check. Go someplace else and do what you want to."

This is what Mr. Big Bucks will usually do, pastors: He won't come to church for a while. He usually won't speak to you, but if he does, he'll say, "You don't *respect* me. You don't *love* me." He'll start crying — and then growling. Sometimes he'll get angry. (Notice these are all symptoms of control!)

He'll say things like, "Who do you think you are, coming into our town? I was here long before you were ever voted in as pastor!"

Here's something you all need to know: You don't *vote* pastors in; God *sets* them in the church. Furthermore, the pastor — not the sheep — is the undershepherd of that congregation. The elders and deacons are to give the pastor counsel and advice, but he is not obligated to always follow this advice if the Spirit of God leads otherwise.

Power Goes to a Novice's Head

Problems arise when you place an immature person such as Mr. Big Bucks into a leadership position in the local church. (1 Tim. 3:6.) His new position as elder, deacon, Sunday School teacher, or whatever may go straight to his head, and a controlling spirit may begin to influence him.

Then he'll begin to brag, "I'm in the leadership of this church. I'll do what I want. I'm a special person." No, you're not a special person, Mr. Big Bucks. You're a servant of all in your new position. You're not Mr. It; you're Mr. *Helps.*

Soon, however, Mr. Big Bucks starts griping and telling the pastor what to sing and what not to sing and what else to do or not do.

The pastor should remove him from the board immediately until he can grow up and learn how to be a gentleman.

I had an interesting experience with one of these types once. He was a typical Mr. Big Bucks. He offered me money if I would get up and *retract* what I had just preached about removing proud board members! I had said, "If a deacon or an elder cannot flow, remove him from the board."

Using Money To Control the Preacher

Mr. Big Bucks said, "I don't think that was right, and I'll give you some money if you'll stand up and retract that statement, because it will cause problems in this church."

I replied, "I won't retract it, because it's right. But you can give me the money anyway." He didn't give me the money. I found out later that *he* was the problem in that church!

He wanted me to retract that statement and and the anointed words that convicted people of their sin. *He wanted to see if he could manipulate me.*

People often come up to me after a service and start arguing and griping. They want me to withdraw something I've said. If I'm wrong about something, I'll apologize. If I've said something that's not right, I'll retract the statement. However, I won't withdraw from the anointing, and I won't apologize for being right. The truth is the truth. When I stand with the truth, I'm right with God and I'm right with the people.

9
Control by Children

Children who dominate and control the lives of their parents also must be dealt with.

I have visited unhappily in homes where the children clearly "rule the roost." They've never been taught either to respect their elders or to share. Such children whine, pout, scream, and cry — and if they aren't the center of attention, they throw a fit!

If parents allow a child to act like this at an early age and never deal with the problem, their future with that child will be hell. (Prov. 22:6.)

My worst illustration of this kind of control is a true case I witnessed in the nation of Sweden.

A couple came to me at the church where I was preaching and said, "Our daughter is possessed by devils."

I turned to the pastor and said, "Pastor, if this is a true case and the girl really wants to get free, I'll pray for her. But if she doesn't, I don't want to waste my time."

I said this because if you want your devils, you may keep them. God will never violate your free will.

The couple brought their daughter to the church. It was wild! They all came running out of the car.

One thing you must never do when devils start manifesting is get flustered. Stay calm and do what you know needs to be done. Be led by the Spirit. You'll win, because the Greater One dwells within you.

So they brought this girl into the church. She started yakking at me, so I grabbed her and said, "Come out of her!" We got all the spirits out of her but one — the major controlling spirit.

Then I began to question her parents about their home life. They told me a fantastic story, but it is absolutely true.

This girl's date didn't pick her up the night of her high school prom. From that day forward, she has done nothing but watch television and drink soft drinks.

She's now in her late twenties. She never cleans her bedroom, never washes her clothes, refuses to get a job — and her parents serve her the soft drinks.

After they told me this, I thought, "You've got to be kidding!" They weren't kidding.

The parents had to leave retirement and go back into the working world to put money into a savings account so that when they die, this girl can continue to drink soft drinks and watch TV.

I thought, "You've got to be crazy! What's wrong with your head?"

"You Just Don't Understand"

The parents saw my shocked expression. They said, "Well, you just don't understand."

I understood very clearly that they were pitifully ignorant of the devil's devices. There is nothing wrong with their daughter, either physically or mentally. Nothing. She is a perfect specimen of a human being.

I even asked the parents, "Is there anything wrong with her mentally?" They said, "No."

And when the girl spoke to me, she spoke as a perfect, intelligent human being — until the evil spirits talked through her.

I told her, "Well, I can't cast this last spirit out, because you're serving it." She liked it because it was catering to her flesh.

I told her parents, "This may sound like a strange thing to do, but the Spirit of God prompted me to tell you to do it: Pack your daughter's clothes, put them on your front porch, and push her out there. And don't let her back into your home until she wakes up and promises to change!"

They wailed, "Oh, oh, oh — we can't do *that*! You don't understand. She needs us. Oh..."

I said, "I thought you wanted her to be set free."

A Chain of Control

I began to see that the controlling spirit in her had gotten hold of her parents too. As I continued to deal with this situation, I learned that three other people in that church were involved in this chain of control!

The controlling spirit that was in the daughter got onto the parents, and from the parents it went onto these three friends. For about a year and a half, the friends had gone to this family's home twice a week, cooked dinner for them, and cleaned their whole house — all because of this girl who did nothing but drink soft drinks and watch TV! *It was a chain of control.*

I know some of you may think, "I just can't believe that," but these things do happen in the world.

This story illustrates how control works in a girl who is perfectly normal mentally and physcially — not spiritually — because she never recovered from that one incident of rejection. The devil got in there, grabbed her, and made her control her whole family as well as three women from the church.

I told these women, "You've got your own homes and children to care for. Here you are taking care of a young adult who does nothing but drink soft drinks and watch TV."

The girl had become so lazy that she eventually slept on the couch and never even went into her bedroom.

That's called EVIL SPIRITS!

That's called CONTROL!

Why would parents waste their lives and leave retirement to put money in a bank account to keep their daughter in laziness? And why were they so caught up in it that they got upset with me when I told them what they needed to do to see their daughter be set free?

I said, "You don't *have* to do that for your daughter. She's not handicapped. She's not a mental case. She's got evil spirits, and she's lazy!"

"Oh, you don't understand the whole situation."

You hear a lot when you confront controlling spirits.

"I do too. You're being controlled by evil spirits, and you need to get free!"

There was nothing further I could do. The daughter didn't want to be free from controlling spirits, and neither did the parents.

10
Control by Spouses

An overbearing husband destroys the life of his wife and children. An overbearing wife destroys the life of her husband and children.

That's why your children want to leave home when they get to the age of 16 or even younger! If you don't leave room for your children to experience joy outside of your parental authority — without your always breathing down their necks — you will have problems with them.

No, I don't mean that your children should be able to do whatever they want to do! You need to understand this message in the Spirit so you may achieve balance in your life. People who don't have balance in their life slide into the errors of carnality or superspirituality.

"Submit, Submit, Submit!"

Some men who have no spiritual balance in their lives turn their wives into weary, battered nothings. These are the husbands who are always yelling, "Submit, submit, submit!"

Some of these hurt and wounded women decided they had to protect themselves, and they became involved in the Women's Liberation Movement. Some joined because of ignorant, insensitive husbands who were always yelling, "Submit, submit, submit..."

On the other hand, some women are just as selfish as these men. I met a pastor's wife in the Midwest who does nothing but drink soft drinks and watch soap operas. She won't cook breakfast for her children, help them get off to school, or make any effort to clean house. She doesn't believe any of these tasks are her job.

If a husband and a wife would flow together in the Spirit, there would be no question of, "Whose job is this and whose job is that?" When there is love in a marriage, there will be mutual consideration for each other. The partners won't be selfish; they'll help each other.

The Development of a Controller

On the other hand, if one of the marriage partners thinks he (or she) is "the big it," he may become a controller. And if his mate isn't strong enough or bold enough to stand up and confront him, she and the children will end up being controlled by him.

He'll strut around like he owns the world. His wife, on the other hand, will be drained and listless — old before her time — and usually not dressed properly.

Children who grow up in this kind of a controlling, negative home life act the same way: They don't care how they dress, and they don't care if they succeed in school. They are the same way at home: They're dominated — controlled — with no security. They, too, have lost their human dignity.

The controlled wife doesn't become a helpmeet in such a marriage; she becomes a slave mate. And that's got to stop.

There is true, biblical submission of a wife toward her husband. That kind of submission is of God, but it's nothing like the submission that is demanded by a selfish companion. You lazy men ought to get up and go clean the table. Go out there and teach your son how to be a man, not a homosexual.

I've met women who can't do anything unless their husband approves of it. Otherwise, he'll get mad. They're afraid to breathe. They live in a circle that's limited by the things their husband allows them to do. That's not having fun together; that's being a robot! All these women can say is, "Whatever you want, dear."

Portrait of a Control Victim

When I preached once in the Northwest, I met a woman who was, unfortunately, a perfect example of a control victim.

Before the service that night, I was sitting at my book table in the back of the church, because I like to talk with people.

I watched this woman enter the church. She was pushing three children under 5 years of age ahead of her like a flock of geese. They were just toddlers, and you know how little toddlers are. They were doing everything all at the same time: screaming, hollering, laughing, amd crying — the whole works. If you have this many children, it takes both parents to handle them, but she was trying to do it alone.

Then I saw the door shut behind a man who had a mean look on his face. I really look at people: I x-ray them! I find out about them. What I saw shocked my spirit.

My spirit went "bong!" — like a bell. I thought, "Something's wrong. Maybe he's oppressed."

The woman really had her hands full, so I walked down the aisle and helped her take the children's coats off. She didn't know I was the preacher. She said, "I wonder where my husband is? Oh, there he is!"

Guess who the husband was? The man who had walked through the door and caused my spirit to go off like an alarm: "THERE'S SOMETHING WRONG, SOME-THING WRONG, SOMETHING WRONG."

He had already found a seat. He didn't even stand up to help with the children. He just pulled his knees back for his wife and children to pass through on their way to their seats. One child "escaped" and started running down the aisle. I picked him up like a sack of potatoes and plopped him in his father's lap, saying, "Here's your child."

I noticed the wife didn't have nice clothes, and the children didn't have nice clothes, but the man was wearing a nice suit.

Controllers Like To Be Served

Controllers try to act like God, because *controlling spirits make people serve their needs and their wants.* They are never considerate of you. This is the hardest thing to get a controller to understand, because he thinks he's so wonderful and so right. He also thinks he loves everybody, because everybody serves *him.* (His idea is totally false, of course.)

I preached a sermon on control that night, and to be honest with you, I preached it to this woman. She came up in the prayer line afterwards.

When I laid my hands on her head and began to pray for her, I felt a "reaction" in her husband, even though he was still back in the congregation. I thought, "Well, we've got a big one here tonight! This is major controlling spirit."

So I grabbed the woman's head again, and I wasn't going to budge this time, because she wanted to be free. She whispered, "I need help. Your'e the first preacher who has let me know what I'm in. I thought that's the way we were supposed to be, but then I saw that other people's marriages were not like mine."

She wasn't talking about "keeping up with the Jonses" as far as material things are concerned; she was talking about a normal interaction between husband and wife: loving each other, holding hands, taking care of their children together — enjoying life together. That's what you got married for. You shouldn't have to live with a bump on a log!

As I was praying for her, she got in the Spirit and began to get free. Her face began to glow. But then something hit her soul and went "bong!" It was her husband's controlling spirit reacting.

I told her, "Keep your head quiet. Don't think. Just flow. God says He wants you to be free." It was 30 minutes before she was able to keep her freedom in the Spirit.

Leaders Should Deal With Controllers

The leaders in that church should have dealt with this problem. We are brothers and sisters, and when there is a situation as bad as this one, and it goes on and on, you elders or deacons should help the pastor confront it and restore liberty and peace to that home. It's part of your job.

Don't advertise the fact that you're dealing with it; just do it. The husband will blow up at first (any evil spirit will blow up when you confront it), but deal with the problem with love and firmness — in the power of the Holy Spirit.

Remember: *You can't fight control only in the natural, because it is a spiritual force.*

11

How To Be Free From Control

There is freedom for those who are bound by control. Whether you are the controller or the person being controlled, you *can* be set free!

Regardless of the *degree* of control you're under, you need to be set free, because you can't live a happy, normal life if you're being controlled by someone else.

How do you break the power of control? *It all boils down to breaking your habit of unnatural expectations toward another person.* You must make yourself break the habit. You must change your habits — and it's difficult for people to do that.

Steps Toward Freedom

If you're a person who is in a controlling situation, here are some steps you can take to get out of this situation.

1. *Recognize that you are controlled.*

Let's review some of the ways you can know if you're being controlled by someone.

When you're around the controller, you're not yourself. You feel intimidated, and you grow increasingly unhappy around him or her. You wish your friendship were as free and happy as other people's.

You feel insecure and inadequate when you try to do new things on your own. Your hopes can be totally dashed and your mind thrown into confusion and instability when your controller makes just one negative statement, such as, "I don't think you can do that."

You feel obligated to spend time with that person, even though he has no consideration for your schedule or lifestyle.

As soon as you return from a pleasant outing with friends, your controller, because he was not invited, feels threatened and attacks you. He may try to "spiritualize" his attack by saying, "I've been in the Spirit, and I know what went on." He will then list things that aren't true, and if you aren't careful, you'll agree with him.

When you're pulled between two opinions, yours and the controller's, you feel obligated to agree with the controller. You lose your human dignity to the point where you're careless about the way you look and you no longer desire to be successful in life. You feel and look exhausted and listless.

2. *Recognize how that person controls you.* Is it through guilt, obligation, anger, tears, frustration, confusion, or the other things we've studied?

3. *Write down the corrections you will need to make in your thought patterns and actions to stop control from happening in your life.*

For example, if the controller controls you through silence, learn not to respond to silence. Don't feel guilty when the controller doesn't speak to you for two weeks. Go on and enjoy life, and let that person have the most miserable time of his or her life, because silence is no longer an effective method to control you.

Often a husband won't speak to his wife (or vice versa) because she did something that he didn't agree with. He uses this childish weapon to punish her instead of discussing the problem like an adult and resolving it so they can live in peace. Personally, I don't understand how people can live with this kind of strife in their homes.

Disharmony Hinders the Spirit

If even a tiny "irk" occurs among my ministerial team, we deal with it and get rid of it immediately, because *the Holy Spirit will not flow through a clogged pipe!*

When you're grieved and hurt, the Holy Spirit can't speak or heal through you. You must be clean to be used by Him.

Another way a controller may try to control you is through words of failure, saying, "You're not educated. You don't know how to do that."

Remind the controller that people thought that Einstein was mentally retarded as a child, and that Abraham Lincoln suffered nothing but defeats and setbacks for years before he became a successful politician. Some of the greatest successes in life were people who didn't have any education. So don't be intimidated.

A controller may even threaten you. Sometimes he'll use this threat: "If you don't do what I say, I'm going to leave you!" You should reply, "Good. Do it!" It will shock him! Of course, exercising any type of strength like this will cause the controller to become very aggressive.

Never be intimidated by anyone. The Greater One lives in you and you're important to God, so you may attack the evil spirits and remind them of this.

Find Scriptures for your battle. Matthew 4:10 is a good one. The devil came to Jesus and said, **. . . fall down and worship me**, and Jesus answered, **Get thee hence, Satan: for it is written, Thou shalt worship the Lord thy God, and him only shalt thou serve.**

Control Equals Idolatry!

When people who are controlled become secure in their relationships with controllers, this amounts to idolatry.

87

That controller of yours has become your god! And you, the controllee, have become the controller's god! That's idolatry. Matthew 4:10, which we just read, is a scripture that will cut this control.

You need to deal with control, because both of you are miserable anyway. Why don't you just get things right with God? To do this, you'll have to learn to pray and break the controlling spirit and all the controlling spirit's "brother" spirits, such as fear, guilt, obligation, confusion, and frustration.

When you say, "I break control," that doesn't mean that you won't experience *loneliness*. Those controlling spirits will storm out of your life, and you'll be left sitting there all by yourself.

The first thing that will hit you is *guilt*, followed by the *fear* that you can't make it on your own. You'll think, "What am I going to do now?"

Don't give up. Stop in your tracks and say, "Devil, move, in Jesus' Name! I break your power. Get off me. You're a liar!" Keep using your authority to rebuke guilt and fear in Jesus' Name (1 Tim. 2:7).

And don't call the controller back, because if he ever comes back, your situation will be worse than it was before!

Control: A Spiritual Problem

Realize that control is not just a natural psychological problem; it is also a *spiritual* problem. As we noted earlier, human nature is naturally controlling, but when control becomes unnatural, it's demonic, and you must learn to fight it — *every day*.

I don't care if you feel like you're no longer under guilt or fear. When you get up in the morning, make sure the first thing you do is to tell those controlling spirits to leave you alone. Break their powers — tell them to go from you in Jesus' Name. Pray in tongues. Quote Scripture to those spirits and make them obey you.

The next time you see the controller, he or she won't speak to you, because you haven't called or hunted him down and asked for help. But don't you dare feel guilty and try to make up with him. *You just won your freedom, so enjoy it!*

First comes this initial break from the controlling person. After you're strong in the Spirit and you know your heart is right, you can take the last step in your complete deliverance from control: *confronting the controller.*

The Battle of Confrontation

You've got to be strong to do enter this "battle to end the war," because controlling people are not the most logical people to deal with.

You must say, "You've controlled me this way, this way, and this way. I love you, but these things will no longer work in my life. You must change, or we can no longer be friends." Bam!

When you do this, several things are likely to happen. As soon as you accuse the person of controlling you, he'll protest, "Not me. I *love* you. I did all of that for your benefit. Do you mean to tell me that you don't appreciate what I've done for you?"

If you're not careful, you'll say, "Oh, I'm sorry. I'm wrong. You have done so much for me."

Then he'll start crying, "You're rejecting me. Look at all I've done for you. You don't like me anymore."

If you aren't careful, you'll slip from your stand in the *Spirit* into the *soulish realm,* which is an emotional realm. The controller will continue, "You know I love you, and we have to work this out." And you'll cry and say, "Oh, I know." And you'll be back in the clutches of control again!

If tears don't work, the controller will try anger. He'll switch back and forth from jealousy, to pride, to control, to fear, and so forth. No human being could change emotions so quickly; it's the controlling spirits in him reacting. If you're really strong in God, you can sit there and call the spirits by name as they are reacting.

Know this: You're in a war; you're not on vacation. If you're weak, you'd better have a group of prayer warriors backing you in prayer when you go into this battle of confrontation.

And when you get home after the confrontation, don't sit at your kitchen table and drink a cup of coffee and meditate about what has just happened. Don't think about it at all! Close your mind off. Instead, walk around and pray in tongues.

The Devil Shows Up When the Power Does

And don't wait for something dramatic to occur to get set free from control. You are going to need to be free and stable in the days ahead, because *when the supernatural power of God falls, the devil will show up and attack at the same time.*

Christians think that when the Holy Spirit falls, everything is wonderful (which it is) and there are no problems. The latter, unfortunately, is not always so. Christians fail to understand that the devil will show up and attack at the same time. Being ignorant of that fact will cause major problems for you.

For example, when the Azusa Street revival was going strong in 1906 and 1907, manifestations of witchcraft occurred in the same meetings! When the Holy Spirit was moving, some people got off in the flesh. That's one of the reasons why the Azusa Street Revival ended before its time.

The Price of the New Move

As I have often stated, the Word of Faith Movement has ended, and the new move has begun. However, this new move of God has come as far as it's going to come to this earth; now we must go out to meet it in the spiritual realm.

How can we can get into this new move of God's Spirit? We can get there through prayer, persistence, and commitment. We also must be real with God, not flaky.

Just be "you" with God, and enjoy being yourself instead of trying to be someone you're not. God does not work through fakes.

Comfort zones are of the flesh. If you've found a place in God where you're comfortable, and you no longer pray or do more than what you normally do, you are in the flesh. You may protest, "But I pray in tongues and worship God." If you don't continue to press on, you will become "religious."

There are people in every church who do not want to go on with God. They're not willing to pay the price to go on. That's why a sense of conflict will seem to be in the air in these churches. That atmosphere is not caused by a lack of prayer or desire toward God in the hearts of most of the congregation; it is caused by those who prefer to stay in their own little rut rather than go on with God.

Those of you who want to go on with God may have to pay a price: You may have to make the very difficult decision to turn loose of friends, associates, or even relatives who do not choose to go on with God and will fight your doing so.

You will continue to love them, pray for them, communicate with them, and visit them; however, with love and firmness, you will not allow them to hinder or dissuade you from going on with God.

If you are not willing to pay this price and deal with controlling or lukewarm people, you will not go on into the new move of God, even though your heart is yearning to do so.

In conclusion: *If Christians don't learn to discern the enemy's tactics, such as his use of controlling spirits, he'll surely try to stop them from charging into the freshness of God's presence!*

12
Prayer for Freedom

Father, we thank You for this message on the problem of control. We give You the glory for it.

I thank You, Father, that You want to set people free from control. I send the Word of God and I break the power of controlling spirits in Jesus' Name. Satan, Loose them and let them go free in Jesus' Name.

I thank You, Father, that the sick are now being healed by your power.

I thank You, God, that you are giving people revelations about their circumstances, so they may know what to do to get free. And please help that person who doesn't want to be free.

Father, I thank You that not one person feels we're against him or her.

Let the Word begin to divide the truth from the false and bring forth freedom in people's lives, so their homes may be full of the presence, power, and joy of God.

We ask this in Jesus' Name. Amen!

About the Author

Roberts Liardon was born in Tulsa, Oklahoma. He was born again, baptized in the Holy Spirit, and called to the ministry at the age of eight, after being caught up to heaven by the Lord Jesus.

Roberts was powerfully commissioned by the Lord to study the lives of God's great men and women ministers, to know why they succeeded and why they failed. The following six years were spent in preparation for that calling and for the vision which God had given him.

In his teens, Roberts began preaching and teaching in various churches — denominational and non-denominational alike — Bible colleges, and universities. He has traveled extensively in the United States and Canada over the past few years.

Roberts' missions outreaches have taken him to Africa, Europe, and Asia. Ministering the Gospel with great anointing from God and the power of the Holy Spirit, Roberts challenges people to walk in the Spirit.

Roberts encourages people to receive the salvation of God and to follow Him. Through his ministry around the world, many people have accepted God's call to yield themselves as vessels for the work of the Kingdom.

Books by Roberts Liardon

I Saw Heaven

Success in Life and Ministry

The Invading Force

The Quest for Spiritual Hunger

The Price of Spiritual Power

Breaking Controlling Powers

Videos by Roberts Liardon

I Saw Heaven

Stirring Up The Gifts of God

*Available from your local bookstore
or by writing:*

Harrison House • P.O. Box 35035 • Tulsa, OK 74153